The supercharged Auburn Speedster of 1936, a classic of its day.

GREAT
AMERICAN
CARS

A 1932 V12 powered Auburn Boat-Tail,
a forerunner of the classic Speedster.

GREAT AMERICAN CARS

JONATHAN WOOD

GALLERY BOOKS
An Imprint of W. H. Smith Publishers Inc.
112 Madison Avenue
New York City 10016

This book was devised and produced by Multimedia Publications (UK) Ltd.

Editor: Jeff Groman
Production: Arnon Orbach
Design: Brian Harris
Picture Research: Paul Snelgrove and
Paul Dowswell

ISBN 0 8317 3983 5

First published in the United States of America, 1985 by Gallery Books, an imprint of W.H.Smith Publishers Inc., 112 Madison Avenue, New York, NY 10016. Typesetting by Front Page Graphics, London. Originated by D. S. Colour International Ltd, London. Printed in Italy by New Interlitho Spa, Milan.

CONTENTS

INTRODUCTION

If Europe gave birth to the motor car then America certainly taught the world how to build it. Almost from birth its automobile industry set the pace in manufacturing techniques, and the Curved Dash Oldsmobile of 1901 has the distinction of being the first mass produced car

The theme was taken up by Henry Ford with his Model T, and the rest of the world followed in the Tin Lizzie's wheel tracks. Introduced in 1908 and mass produced from 1914, the Model T was so successful that it was estimated in 1919 that one car in two was a Ford! Output peaked in 1922 and the model lasted until 1927, by which time over 16 million models had been built. It made Ford the first motoring billionaire and underlined the genius of American marketing, which took a luxury item and streamlined the production process so that it could then be sold at a price that the man in the street, or on the farm, could afford.

Not that Ford had things all his own way. It was in 1908, the year of the Model T's arrival, that William Durant established his General Motors Corporation, with Buick as its mainstay and soon to be augmented by the Cadillac and Oldsmobile marques. With GM it was Buick that challenged the value for money Model T, while the corporate high-quality low-production car was soon to emerge as the Cadillac, precision built by that master of interchangeable parts, Henry Leland. The finely engineered Cadillac V8 of 1914 was not America's first V8 by any means but the quality of its design and execution was such that it immediately stood head and shoulders above its contemporaries. The model's arrival established a prestigious momentum that continues to this day. Rivalling the Cadillac at the top end of the market was Jesse Vincent's Twin Six Packard of 1915, the world's first series production V12 model. It was to establish the make as one of America's most exclusive, and the firm's reputation for the quality and refinement of its engineering was assured.

Yet another firm that preferred exclusiveness to quantity was Lincoln, established after Henry Leland and his son Wilfred had left Cadillac in 1917. Not unnaturally they opted for an impressive V8 engine model but soon found themselves in financial difficulties and were bailed out, in 1922, by the master of mass

Half a century of progress. Above: the Curved Dash Oldsmobile, the world's first mass produced car; this is a 1904 example. Left: the Model T Ford, the world's best selling car until it was usurped by the Volkswagen Beetle; a 1915 car is shown. Far left: luxury from Duesenberg, a 1934 Model J with Victoria body by Rollston. Above left: Ford's first unsuccessful bid for the sporting market; a 1956 two seater Thunderbird.

production, Henry Ford. The Lelands soon departed, however, and the direction of the firm's affairs became the responsibility of Ford's eldest son Edsel.

The 1920s were dominated by a furious sales battle between Henry Ford and General Motors, the latter aggressively directed by the trained corporate mind of Alfred Sloan Jr. from 1920. In 1917 a temporarily vanquished William Durant had returned to take control of the Corporation, bringing with him his own Chevrolet marque. Although Durant was finally ousted from control in 1920, Chevrolet was to go on to become the world's best selling make. The Ford T's replacement, the Model A, took Henry back to the top of the production tree in 1929 and 1930 but during the following year General Motors and Chevrolet moved ahead and, apart from a few exceptional years, stayed there.

The affairs of Errett Lobban Cord and the Cord Corporation were far removed from such conflicts, though the firm, with its trio of Auburn, Cord and Duesenberg marques, produced some of America's most visually impressive cars of the inter-war years. Auburn is best remembered for its famous Speedster two seaters, which for many typify the heady, booming America of the 1920s. The low, stylish front wheel drive Cord, by contrast, arrived in 1929, the same year as the Wall Street crash, and from thereon the Corporation slid inexorably into decline. Before this happened, the front wheel drive 810 Cord appeared in 1935, setting a stylistic trend that was to endure until the 1950s. But the greatest of all the Cord triumvirate was Duesenberg. Fred and August

Duesenberg's race-bred cars began with the Model A in 1920, but Cord was determined to rival Europe's best: the result was the renowned Model J of 1928 with the memorable 'Duesenberg look' created by Gordon Buehrig's stylistic abilities. Alas, all three makes perished with the collapse of the Cord Corporation in 1937.

All the principal car makers — Ford, General Motors and Chrysler (established in 1923 and destined to move center stage with its low priced Plymouth marque from 1928) — survived the 1930s depression years. However, Ford, still managed by the ageing, obstinate Henry Ford, was probably in the worst shape by the time America entered World War II in 1941. During the Depression, car output plummeted from 4.4 million in 1929 to 1.1 million in 1932, but the increased competition in the shrinking

---

Above: Ford's success story of the 1960s, the Mustang, aimed foursquare at the young buyer. This is a GT-350 fastback by Carroll Shelby with 289 cid (4.8 liter) V8 engine. **Right:** outstanding styling from Gordon Buehrig, the extraordinary front wheel drive Cord 810. This is a 1936 S10 convertible Phaeton.

market also stimulated the evolution of vehicle styling. The boxy themes of the 1920s, were replaced by new shapes with an emphasis on horizontals rather than verticals. In addition, the new science of aerodynamics was reflected in such vehicles as the Chrysler Airflow, Pierce Silver Arrow show cars and the Lincoln Zephyr.

A curious paradox of the 1930s was that there was a spate of V12 and V16 engined models, with Cadillac setting the pace and Pierce-Arrow, Marmon, Packard and Lincoln following. But only Packard and Lincoln, the latter underwritten by Ford, survived into the post-war years.

Throughout World War II the automobile companies played a crucial role in turning America into an arsenal of liberty. With the coming of peace, their 1942 models were dusted off, but in 1947 the Big Three car makers were joined by a new challenger in the mass production markets: the Kaiser and Frazer makes from the newly formed Kaiser-Frazer Corporation. For a time the gamble seemed to pay off, with the new firm attaining five per cent of new car sales in 1948, but two years later the founders parted company and the firm was renamed Kaiser Motors. It was in 1953 that Kaiser bought Willys-Overland, once a front runner in the mass production markets of the 1920s, and in 1955 the firm ceased building private cars to concentrate on the Jeep. Also worthy of mention, if only because it was so extraordinary, was the Tucker, another new post-war make. It was powered by a flat six cylinder engine which had been designed for use in Bell helicopters positioned in the rear of this curious sedan. As if this wasn't enough there was rubber suspension, disc brakes and central headlamp that turned with the steering. Not surprisingly, few Tuckers were built and the make only lasted until 1948.

But of all the new models that appeared in 1948, the beginning of the post-war era, the most famous were the Series 62 Cadillacs, with distinctive tailfins inspired by the Lockheed P38 fighter. As a stylistic feature it was to be widely imitated in the 1950s, along with a surfeit of chrome plate that was to mirror a decade of expansion, prosperity and national self assurance.

Yet another facet of the helter-skelter 1950s was the almost universal provision of the V8 engine. Since before World War II it had been the almost exclusive preserve of the low-production high-cost market sector, though Henry Ford offered the world the first cheap mass produced L head V8 in 1932. But it wasn't until the post-war era that other manufacturers followed suit, relying on their existing straight six and eight L head units. Oldsmobile's overhead valve, high compression V8 arrived in 1949 and two years later, in 1951, Chrysler introduced its FirePower V8 with hemispherical combustion chambers. It soon became known, more informally, as the 'Hemi', and with 180 bhp from 331 cid (5.4 liters) it was the most powerful V8 of its year, with plenty left in reserve. It comes as no surprise to find that by 1955 Ford, Chevrolet and Plymouth, the traditional bottom line trio, were all offering overhead valve V8s. Those firms that procrastinated suffered terminal fates. Kaiser-Frazer only offered a six throughout its eight year production life, and Hudson and Packard — who eventually did take the plunge — were too late in deciding and were squeezed out by the big battalions. Hudson disappeared from the market in 1957 and Packard vanished in 1958 in the wake of an ill fated merger with Studebaker. That old established American make ceased production in 1966, having transferred its manufacturing operations to Canada two years previously.

The 1950s were also a time when the American car makers began to respond to the influx of European sports cars. Of the Big Three, General Motors was the first to respond: in 1953 it

Above right: A Woodie amongst the trees, a 1948 Chrysler Town and Country convertible coupe. Far right: when fins and chrome were all the rage in the 1950s, a 1959 Pontiac Bonneville. Right: 1937 Lincoln Zephyr, the first medium priced Lincoln with V12 engine, which saved the marque.

introduced the glass fiber-bodied Chevrolet Corvette which, despite an uncertain start, has been an integral part of the American motoring scene ever since. Ford's response was the two seater Thunderbird, but sales were disappointing and in 1958 the name, too good to be allowed to lapse, was transferred to a more popular four seater line.

By the next decade the tailfins had all but disappeared, though there were significant changes taking place under those commodious hoods. The Muscle Car era had arrived in earnest, usually landmarked by the Pontiac GTO of 1964, following the industry's widespread introduction of V8 engines. Cubic capacities and horse power outputs soared, top speeds rocketed but so did gas consumption . . .

It was also 1964 that marked the arrival of the fastest selling car, certainly in its first year, in the history of the American automobile industry. This was the Ford Mustang, aimed squarely at the youth boom that came of age in the 1960s and master-minded by Lee Iacocca, General Manager of the Ford division.

Although stringent government regulations concerning vehicle construction and engineering were still in the future, the arrival in 1965 of Ralph Nader's *Unsafe at Any Speed*, with its articulate criticisms of American car design in general and the Chevrolet Corvair in particular, caused more than a flurry in corporate dove cotes. It was to foreshadow safety and exhaust emission requirements, which came into force in 1968 and were to radically affect the home industry and the foreign exporters who were so dependent for vehicles sales in the vast American market place. This federal directive was fortified by the 1973 energy crisis and, as a result, all US manufacturers were directed to produce by 1978 a model range which returned an overall gas consumption of 20 miles per gallon.

The downturn in the world economies in the wake of rising oil prices and the growing popularity of smaller cars resulted in America, which had been the world's foremost car maker since 1908, ceding its pole position to Japan in 1980. Since then America has hit back with smaller, front wheel drive cars, though the thirsty V8, so long synonymous with the New World's automotive approach, seems doomed to obscurity. And, in 1984 the industry was, once again, the world's largest.

No matter. What better time to look back and enter the world of the idiosyncratic Model T Ford, the fabulous Cadillacs and Duesenbergs, the be-finned and chromed Oldsmobiles and Chevrolets, while not forgetting the era when Muscle was the Master.

Left: Buick's long running Riviera, this one dates from the 1963 introductory year. Far left: as immortalized in the song, a 1957 Chevrolet, in this instance a Bel Air convertible. Above left: front wheel drive from Cadillac, a 1976 Eldorado special edition convertible.

OLDSMOBILE

Best selling buggy

The world's first mass produced car was a robust little single cylinder buggy: the Curved Dash Oldsmobile. Ransom Eli Olds grew up in Lansing, the state capital of Michigan, where his father ran an engineering and machine shop. After producing a three wheeled steam car in 1891, five years later, Olds produced his first gas buggy, which soon became a familiar sight on the Lansing streets. With the backing of two local businessmen, Olds transferred his operations to Detroit, where the firm initially concentrated on stationary gas and petrol engines. Then, in 1899, they decided to enter the automobile business, launching a $1,250 car and some electric cars. This produced an $80,000 loss in 1900; Olds then decided to go to the other automotive extreme and came up with the idea of a simple, cheap buggy weighing just 500 lb and selling for $500. As it turned out, the Curved Dash Runabout that resulted weighed in at 700 lb and sold for $650. It had a single cylinder 91 cid (1.5 liters) engine with two speed epicyclic gearbox and chain drive to the rear axle. The prototype was completed in 1901, but in March Olds' Jefferson Avenue factory was burned to the ground. Fortunately, the little buggy was saved. It was taken apart, new drawings were made and it entered production later in the year when 425 examples were sold. Next year the figure spiralled to 2,500, made possible by the rebuilt factory assembling, rather than manufacturing, the car. John and Horace Dodge provided engines and transmissions, along with Leland and Faulconer. In 1903 sales rose to 4,000 and to 5,508 the following year. By this time Olds had left the company to build the Reo car, the name being derived from his initials.

Ransom Olds' Curved Dash, the model that proved to be a salvation for the young company. This is a 1903 example with single cylinder engine and chain drive. Olds soon afterwards left the firm that, in 1908, became part of General Motors.

FORD MODEL T

Henry's world wide car

The car that truly put the world on wheels, the Ford Model T, built between 1908 and 1927 — the most popular car in the history of the automobile until it was overtaken by the Volkswagen Beetle in 1973. The T's production eventually stood at an estimated 16,561,850 and established Henry Ford as the world's foremost car maker. The spidery, angular Ford was deceptively robust and powered by a 176 cid (2.9 liters) four cylinder engine, with detachable cylinder head, an unusual feature for the day. A two speed epicyclic gearbox was fitted while suspension was by transverse springs located by radius rods. The car was mass produced from 1914 in a purpose-built factory at Highland Park, Detroit, and black was the only color available between that year and 1925. Output soared: in 1922 a million Model Ts were built for the first time in one year and production peaked in 1923 when two million were built. The original price had been set at $850 but, with the benefits of mass production, the price progressively fell so that by 1925 a T tourer cost $250. Although electric starting was offered from 1920, the Ford never boasted such up-to-date fittings as front wheel brakes. The car became progressively outdated, with production ceasing in 1927. The factory closed down for six months to re-tool for the Model A, the T's replacement, but Ford's market dominance was lost and from 1931 General Motors and Chevrolet forged ahead. Yet the T's inheritance of low cost cars representing good value for money was to indelibly stamp itself on the Ford Motor Company's products, which are all spiritual heirs of the ubiquitous Tin Lizzie.

The car that not only put the world on wheels but was also mass produced and gave the industry the moving track assembly line. Both these are brass radiatored Ts, a black painted one arrived in 1917. Over 16 million examples were built.

The Model T's distinctive transverse leaf
suspension and high ground clearance,
making it ideal for the heavily rutted
American roads of the day, are well
displayed on this 1915 car.

PACKARD TWIN SIX

Packard takes the lead

The world's first series production V12 was built by Packard and in doing so the firm was to establish a pre-eminence that was to endure until the 1950s. The Packard brothers, James and William, had built their first car in 1899, having bought a Winton the previous year and decided it required improvement. The duo were already running a firm (in Warren, Ohio) which built electrical equipment, and the first Packard was the usual type of Turn of the Century American design — a sparse high-wheeled buggy with single cylinder engine. The firm was taken over by Detroit industrialist Henry B. Joy in 1902, though James Packard remained as Chairman. The first four cylinder Packard, the Model K, appeared in 1903, while a six cylinder car arrived in 1912. But it was the Twin Six that replaced it that gave Packard a reputation for quality and refinement. It was the work of Jesse Vincent, whose engineering qualifications had been limited to International Correspondence School studies in the evenings. He had joined Packard in 1912, though the firm had already been thinking about a larger car prior to his arrival. The resulting 427 cid (7 liters) Twin Six was the first American touring car to be fitted with aluminum, rather than cast iron, pistons; a notable technological first. With Cadillac having just introduced its V8 the two principal rivals for America's luxury market were clearly defined. The Twin Six remained in production until 1923, when it was replaced by a straight eight model, but Packard reverted to a V12 in 1932 and this configuration endured throughout the 1930s.

The car that established Packard as one of America's outstanding makes: the V12 Twin Six. This is an elegant 1922 example; the following year the model was discontinued.

CORD L29

Front wheel drive pioneer

Errett Lobban Cord, who had made his money as a highly successful car salesman, had bought the run-down Auburn company in 1924 and followed this with the purchase of Duesenberg in 1926. In 1929 he formed the Cord Corporation, which by this time included Lycoming engines and Stinson aircraft. That year the Cord name was introduced and the first model, which appeared that August, was a visual triumph. So that he could obtain a low styling look, Cord opted for front wheel drive. The mechanical design was the work of Cornelius van Ranst, who had previously worked for Harry Miller, whose front wheel drive racing cars had made such an impression on the Indianapolis 500 since 1926. Miller patents were incorporated in the design, a 317 cid (5.2 liters) side valve Lycoming engine was reversed in the frame and a de Dion axle, à la Miller, was employed. The Cord Corporation's Al Leamy then produced a low sedan body, made possible by the absence of an intrusive propellor shaft, which caused a worldwide sensation. But the model's timing could not have been worse, since the Wall Street financial crash was only two months away. Also, at $3,000 the L29 was an expensive car, so production only lasted until 1932, by which time 4,400 had been built. Nevertheless this Cord can be regarded as America's first series production front wheel drive car and was to pave the way to an even more exciting model in 1935.

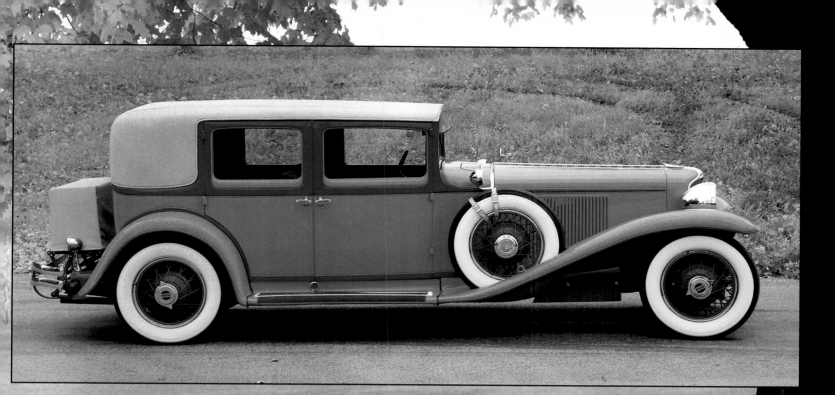

Above, one of Cord's most impressive
creations, the L-29, a front wheel drive car
which permitted a long, low look, and
introduced in 1929. This is a 1931 cabriolet.
Top: variation on a theme; a 1930 sedan.

1931-1936
DUESENBERG J & SJ

Gordon Buehrig became Duesenberg's chief body designer. He began producing some highly individual body styles which were interpreted by such renowned custom body builders as Murphy and Derham, which resulted in the all-important Duesenberg look. But the effects of the Depression cast a shadow across the model's sales and, in an attempt to broaden the car's appeal, a supercharged version, the SJ was introduced in 1932. This necessitated the introduction of external chromed exhaust pipes, which all added to the magic and they also became a popular accessory on the unblown cars. There was also a rare short wheelbase SSJ version but total J series production only amounted to around 470 cars. Duesenberg, alas, disappeared with the collapse of the Cord Corporation in 1937.

Smooth and stylish

Having gained control of Duesenberg in 1926, Errett Lobban Cord recognized that although the Model A was an impressive technical package it lacked the glamor and prestige of the British Rolls-Royce or Hispano-Suiza from France. The outlines of a new, impressive Duesenberg were accordingly hammered out between Cord and Harold Ames, the firm's Vice President, on the former's kitchen table, and were then handed over to the Indianapolis factory to interpret. The outcome was a visual and mechanical triumph. The Lycoming-built 420 cid (6.9 liters) engine had twin overhead camshafts, while its four valves per cylinder echoed the Duesenberg brothers' racing experiences. On announcing the introduction of the Model J in late 1928, its

A magnificent trio of Duesenbergs which underlines Cord's desire to produce America's finest car. Above: Model J with Rollston coachwork. Above right: 1933 SJ with bodywork by Walton. Right: 1936 SJ with English coachwork by Gurney Nutting, all cars courtesy of the Auburn, Cord, Duesenberg Museum.

CADILLAC V16

Luxury and good looks

Cadillac had broken new ground with its V8 engine Model 51 in 1914 and did so again in 1930 with the worlds first series production V16 engined automobile. Details of the new car were given over the radio the second week in December 1929, just two months after the Wall Street crash. The V16 was the flagship of the Cadillac range and the production of such a complex and sophisticated engine was only made possible by General Motors' incomparable resources. Work on the engine had begun in 1927 to the designs of Cadillac engineer Owen Nacker, and the smoothness and silence of the 451 cid (7.4 liters) V16 became legendary. This was due, in part, to the fitting of hydraulic tappets, used for the first time on a General Motors product and subsequently employed by other manufacturers of prestige motor cars such as Packard and Rolls-Royce. The car entered production in 1930 and sales amounted to 3,240 for these first 12 months. But demand fell away as the Depression took hold and from then on annual sales hovered around the 50 mark, with a total of 3,863 cars built, up to the model's demise in 1937. It was replaced by a simpler V16, with side valves instead of overhead ones and around half the number of parts of its predecessor. A mere 511 were built between 1938 and 1940. Mention should be made of a 366 cid (6 liter) V12 introduced soon after the V16 and effectively three-quarters of the larger engine. This remained in production until 1937, by which time 10,821 had been built.

Above: The rare goddess mascot used by Cadillac and made by Ternstedt of Detroit. Available only in 1930/2, this one is on a 1931 car. Above right: a 1933 Cadillac Fleetwood Formal Town Car, once owned by movie star Joan Crawford and, of course, V16 engined. Right: a 1931 V16 model with cabriolet coachwork.

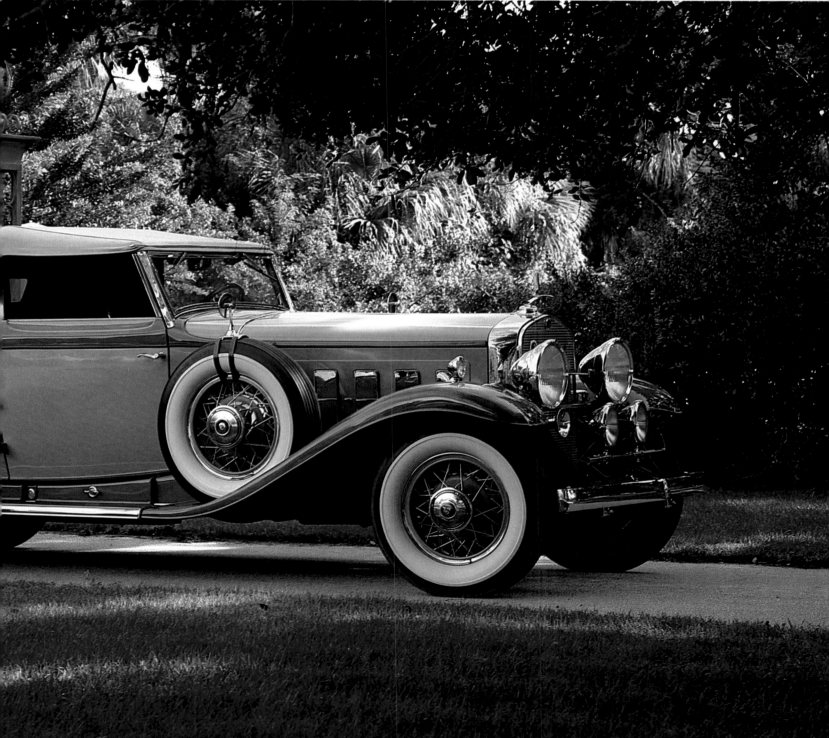

AUBURN V12 SEDANS

Power and silence

With the automobile companies feeling the effects of the Depression years, Errett Lobban Cord decided to offer the cheapest V12 on the market and did so in 1932. The bottom line Standard Coupe of the 12-160 range sold for an incredible $975 and even though prospective purchasers were somewhat alarmed to find that this did not include tires, it still represented remarkable value for money. The 12-160A Custom Twelve was offered with a vacuum operated two speed rear axle from Columbia Gear, a Cord Corporation subsidiary. With the attribute of V12 power and smoothness and this novel rear axle facility, Cord hoped that he would take the V12 market by storm and even the top line Custom Speedster cost only $1275. The all important engine was a 391 cid (6.4 liter) Lycoming built V12. Like its

Cadillac opposite number it was a 45 degree V but whereas the superlative General Motors product boasted overhead valves, the Auburn had almost horizontal ones, not dissimilar to those employed by Packard. This was a progression from the L head layout previously employed and meant that the V12 Auburns were capable of around 100 mph. Yet despite all their attributes the V12s were a sales flop. From selling an impressive 32,301 Auburns in 1931, the firm suffered a slump in demand to 7,939 cars in the following year. The V12 remained available until 1934; thereafter only sixes and eights were on offer. It was in that year Cord departed to England though two years later returned to America to preside over the demise of the Cord Corporation.

Far left: elegance from the Auburn, Cord and Duesenberg stable. A 1932 Auburn Phaeton sedan model 12-161A. Above, the same model and year but different body. This is a sedan version. In both instances the cars are V12 powered.

MARMON V16

Multi cylinder morass

The Indianapolis based Marmon company was always in the forefront of technical developments. Howard C. Marmon, who had gained his mechanical training in the family flour milling machinery business, built his first car in 1902. Two years later, in 1904, came an air-cooled V4 aluminum engined model, though it was replaced by a more conventional T head four in 1908. During World War I service in France, Howard Marmon had the opportunity of studying a 16 cylinder Bugatti aero engine, which fired his enthusiasm for the configuration. In the 1920s a six cylinder line was marketed, though in 1927 there came a 189 cid (3.1 liters) straight eight from which Marmon had already produced an experimental V16, but the V16 that finally arrived in 1931 was a 494 cid (8.1 liters) aluminum unit with wet cylinder liners which mirrored Marmon's preoccupation with lightness and overhead valves. The chassiswork, styled by industrial designer Walter Dorwin Teague, was slightly severe in appearance, which hardly echoed the impressive mechanical specifications. It is difficult to imagine a worse time for a small company to introduce such a sophisticated product. Not only had the market for luxury cars been decimated by the Depression but there were also formidable challenges from the Cadillac V16 and V12 as well as from a variety of V12s from Packard, Lincoln, and Pierce-Arrow. It is no surprise to find that the Marmon Motor Company went out of business in 1933 after 390 examples of its V16 model had been produced.

Below: The model that broke Marmon, the V16 which lasted until 1933. There were also attempts to produce a V12 version but only one prototype was built and Marmon came to the end of the road.

PIERCE SILVER ARROW

Wind cheating show cars

George N. Pierce, who produced bicycles and bird cages, built his first Pierce car in Buffalo, New York, in 1901. The Arrow name made its appearance in 1903 and in 1909 the firm's name was changed to Pierce-Arrow. Thereafter the firm concentrated on six cylinder models, the massive 66 of 1912 of 823 cid (13.5 liters) being America's largest capacity model. The 1920s, however, were less successful and in 1928 Studebaker took the firm over. A new generation of straight eight models was introduced for 1929, while in 1932 came a V12 offered in 396 cid (6.5 liters) and 427 cid (7 liter) forms. It was in that year that Phil Wright (a former General Motors stylist who had already designed a rear engined 'vehicle for the future' for GM, and had subsequently lost his job) sent a clay model of a futuristic design to the home of

Pierce-Arrow's President Roy Faulkner. The executive liked what he saw and sanctioned the production of five V12s featuring Wright's design. Work began on the first car in October 1932 at Studebaker's factory at South Bend, Indiana, under the direction of chief chassisbuilding engineer, James R. Hughes. It was completed in time for the New York Auto Show, which opened on New Year's Day, 1933, where the fastback styling, lack of running boards, spatted rear wheels, concealed door hinges, and integral headlamps caused a sensation. Even though the firm proclaimed: 'Born in the wind tunnel, made by hand', the design had never been near such a facility! A display at the Chicago World Fair later in the year was equally sensational and of the five Silver Arrows sold at $10,000 apiece, no less than four survive. The lines, unfortunately, were not transferred to the production car and by 1938 Pierce-Arrow was no more.

Above: The tragedy of the Pierce Silver Arrow design was that it was never transferred to production cars. The Arrows were individually built, there were five in all, and received rapturous receptions whenever they were exhibited.

PACKARD V12

Cadillac's challenger

Packard's famous Twin Six, introduced in 1915, remained in production until 1923, when it was replaced by a straight eight model. However, in 1930 Cadillac introduced its V16 and V12 models, so Packard subsequently re-activated the engine configuration and Twin Six name for which it was so famous. For its new V12, Packard secured the services of Cornelius van Ranst, who had the engineering of the L29 Cord to his credit. Packard had ambitiously decided to make its new V12 a front wheel drive offering, like the Cord, and a prototype was accordingly produced. Unfortunately there were problems with the trans axle which stripped some of its gear teeth, demanding a complete redesign. But there was neither the time nor the money to embark on such a rethink so the V12, which arrived in 1932, had a conventional transmission. The 439 cid (7.2 liters) engine was also designed by van Ranst, of which the aluminum cylinder heads and near horizontal valves were notable features. The model was initially available with a handsome range of chassiswork from custom chassisbuilders Dietrich; 549 examples sold in the first year of production. About the same numbers were sold in the following 12 months but subsequently things perked up and by the time the V12 was discontinued in 1939 no less than 13,400 had found customers. Although the Twin Six name was only carried in 1932, thereafter being known as the Twelve, mechanical changes were few. Hydraulic brakes only arrived in 1937 (although the front wheel drive prototype had boasted them), and the Safe-T-fleX independent suspension system was introduced in the same year.

With Cadillac setting the pace in the 1930s with V16 and V12 models, Packard had to respond. Below: 1933 Packard Twelve. Initially known, in 1932, as the Twin Six, in memory of its distinguished 1915 forebear, the V12 was subsequently known as the Twelve. Right: the famous pelican mascot fitted on the Twelve and Super Eights.

A reminder that what might be
aerodynamically acceptable may not
always be stylistically so, as Chrysler found
with its 1934 Airflow. It proved a disaster for
the firm and in its introductory year only
10,839 examples were sold. Right, above:
a 1934 example which contrasts with the
hastily re-vamped version, introduced in
1935 which lasted until 1937. This car dates
from the latter year.

Unacceptable aerodynamics

Walter P. Chrysler left General Motors and established the Chrysler Corporation in 1923. This had absorbed Dodge in 1928 and created two new makes, Plymouth and De Soto, the same year. By the early 1930s Chrysler was in third place behind General Motors and Ford in car production. The company's Director of Research was Carl Breer, a graduate of Stanford University and interested in aerodynamics. He got William Earnshaw, a freelance engineer, to investigate vehicle shapes. Following a visit to Orville Wright, Earnshaw went ahead and constructed a small wind tunnel to test wooden models. His results were sufficient for Breer to go ahead and have a large tunnel built, and the results of his experiments showed that the average American car was aerodynamically more efficient going backwards, so he set to work to design a 'back to front' car. The Chrysler Airflow of 1934 was the result. Even today it looks an unusual car, with waterfall radiator, double vertically mounted integral headlights and spatted rear wheels. The engine was forward mounted (sixes and eights were available) in the interests of good weight distribution, and this, along with the unorthodox styling, resulted in public indifference: the Airflow was a sales flop. So for 1935 the model was hastily revamped with a more traditional radiator grille, a rare instance of an evolutionary styling process being arrested and placed in reverse.

AUBURN SPEEDSTER

Two seater to oblivion

Auburn was a run of the mill auto company hailing from Auburn, Indiana, which had been building cars since 1900. However, in 1924 Errett Lobban Cord bought the firm and proceeded to revitalize it. The most memorable of the model line up was a 276 cid (4.5 liters) straight eight, introduced in 1925 and notable for its dual color schemes which followed the line of a belt molding and extended from the sides of the car along the hood, converging on the radiator cap. This evolved into the 115 Model of 1928, the most impressive option being a two seater Speedster, styled by Count Alexis de Sakhnoffsky, with raked windscreen and boat tail which for many epitomized the carefree American spirit of the 1920s.

With the coming of the Depression, Auburn was soon in trouble, though Speedster versions of successive models continued to be built in small numbers. It was the 851 of 1935 that has proved most enduring. Styled by Gordon Buehrig, it followed on from his cost-conscious revamping of the 851 series sedans for 1935. Buehrig then recalled that there were still about 100 Speedster bodies built by the Union City Body Company of Union City, Indiana, left over from a 1933 version. Using this design as a basis, Buehrig obtained a body, cut it in half, designed a new rear portion, restyled the front in line with the revised sedans and introduced external chromed exhaust pipes in the Duesenberg manner. The cars made a considerable visual impact and there was the supercharged 852 of 1936, identical to the 851 except for '852' on its radiator. But the Cord Corporation collapsed in 1937 and Auburn was no more.

The styling talents of Gordon Buehrig are all too evident in the Auburn Speedster. In both these examples the 279 cid (4.5 liter) straight engine has been supercharged, as indicated on the hood sides. Alas, this handsome car was out of step with the austerity of the Depression years and only about 500 examples were built.

1936
FORD V8

Cheap and smooth

Henry Ford's great achievement was to give the world the Model T, but from its demise in 1927 he was never again to dominate the American market. But he had one great, final contribution to make to the evolution of the motor car, and that was the low-cost mass produced V8 introduced in 1932. Until then the V8 had been confined to the exclusive end of the car market, as the superlative designs of Cadillac and Lincoln bore witness. These, like practically every other V8 of their day, were built up by bolting two cast iron cylinder blocks to an aluminium crankcase. But a team of Ford engineers, working in the unlikely surroundings of a replica of Thomas Edison's famous laboratory, came up at Henry's insistence, with an iron V8 that could be cast in one piece, cheapening and simplifying the production process. The 195 cid

(3.2 liters) head V8 sold for $460, which was only $50 more than the four cylinder Model B, introduced the same year. In June 1934 the millionth V8 was produced and such was the appeal of this smooth, reliable engine that the two millionth example was built the following year. This helped Ford to pull ahead of General Motors' Chevrolet as America's top selling make (though GM, with its variety of designs, was in front overall). Nevertheless, the Corporation was back on top in 1936 and it was not until 1959 that Ford again inched ahead. The V8's chassis retained the Model T's archaic transverse leaf suspension and mechanical brakes though these were changed to hydraulics in 1939. The faithful L header soldiered on until 1954, by which time the rest of the industry had produced its own popular V8s, a good 20 years after Henry Ford had shown them how.

Above: The low cost Ford V8, introduced in 1932, did much to bolster Ford sales in the 1930s even though the chassis was Model T derived. This is a 1936 Fordor saloon which was, surprisingly, less popular than the Tudor version.

1936
CORD 810

Buehrig breakthrough

The Cord Corporation had already established a reputation for producing visually impressive cars, as the distinctive Auburns, Cords, and Duesenbergs bore witness. In 1935 it introduced perhaps the most memorable of them all: the Cord 810, an extraordinarily modern offering for its day and styled by the talented Gordon Buehrig. He had been appointed chief body designer for Duesenberg in 1929 but in 1933 had joined General Motors for a brief spell before returning to the Indianapolis company. It was while at GM that Buehrig conceived the idea of creating a highly original four door sedan with an angular hood, dispensing with the conventional radiator and replacing it with two side-mounted units. This design was produced in prototype form in 1934 as a small Auburn-engined Duesenberg, but it was then decided to alter the concept by converting it to front wheel

drive and selling it as a Cord. The 286 cid (4.7 liters) V8 was designed by Forest S. (Bill) Baster, Lycoming's chief engineer, while the gearbox, which lived out in front of the car, was a curious pre-selector electro vacuum device operated by a small lever on the steering column. But the 810's *tour de force* was its bodywork: low with coffin front, pop-up headlamps, concealed door hinges and no running boards. Announced in 1935, there was a four door sedan and two door convertible. In closed form the 810 was expensive at $1,995, and maybe its revolutionary looks were against it, despite the arrival in 1937, of the 812 model, with optional supercharger costing $415. The Cord marque unfortunately sank with the Cord Corporation that year and just 2,320, 810/812 Cords were built; the many survivors bear witness to Gordon Buehrig's genius.

Below: Yet another magnificent but short lived model from the Cord Corporation. This is a 1937 Cord 812. Note the pop up headlights, inspired by the landing lights of the Stimson aeroplane, another firm in the Cord corporate bow.

Above: a 1936 Westchester sedan with Gordon Buehrig, its talented stylist, in attendance.

LINCOLN ZEPHYR

Edsel's V12 savior

When Henry Leland and his son Wilfred left Cadillac in 1917 they established the Lincoln Motor Company, so called because Leland senior had cast his first vote for Abraham Lincoln back in 1864. The first model was a 353 cid (5.8 liters) V8 in the Cadillac manner, introduced in 1922. But the following year the firm ran out of money and was bought by Henry Ford. Soon afterwards the Lelands departed and Henry's son Edsel assumed responsibility for this high-quality low-production car. V8 engines were exclusively offered until 1932, when a V12 of 439 cid (7.2 liters) appeared, with a smaller 378 cid (6.2 liters) version following. But as the luxury market declined, a cheaper model, the Zephyr, appeared for 1936. Its styling had been inspired by a design exercise undertaken by John Tjaarda for Briggs Motor Bodies in 1933 but mildly modified so as not to be too radical, the cool

reception of the Chrysler Airflow no doubt providing its own lessons. The Zephyr's 268 cid (4.4 liters) V12 was cheaply built, compared with earlier Lincoln V12s, and was effectively one and a half Ford V8s. Although there were reliability problems with the engine, Lincoln sales rose from a mere 830 cars in 1935, to 16,509 in 1936, of which no less 14,994 were Zephyrs. The car was priced at $1,320 on its announcement, which reflected its Ford-based mechanics of transverse leaf suspension and mechanical brakes. The model remained in production until 1948, which was the last year a V12 engined Lincoln was available.

A 1940 Lincoln Zephyr with front end re-designed and sharpened by Ford's Eugene Gregorie, also responsible for the fabled Continental. Above: a 1937 example of the model.

LINCOLN CONTINENTAL

Exclusive refinement

Undoubtedly the most memorable and visually impressive of the pre-war Lincolns was the Continental, introduced in 1940. During the 1930s, Edsel Ford had used a number of special bodied cars for his own use and it was in the latter months of 1938, after returning from a visit to Europe, that he decided he wanted a convertible of distinctly European inspiration. Stylist Eugene Turenne Gregorie came up with the idea of using the Lincoln Zephyr chassis. Ford approved his clay model in October 1938 and, in order to speed the process, there was no full sized clay. The body was made by hand by Henry Cornelius, head of Lincoln's body engineering division. A distinctive feature was the spare wheel, carried outboard at the rear of the car and destined thereafter to become a feature of the make. The car was completed in February 1939 and then sent to Edsel's holiday home at Hobe Sound, Florida. It made an immediate and impressive impact with Edsel and his free-spending friends, so it was decided to market the car as a new Lincoln model. A further prototype was built in 1940, fitted with a steering column gear change, the first of the Ford family to feature the layout. Production began in 1940, continued until 1942 and was revived after the war, spanning the 1946-8 period. In the latter year the New York Museum of Modern Art chose the Continental as one of eight cars exhibited for their 'excellence as works of art'. It was a fitting testament to the memory of Edsel Ford, who had died in 1943 at the tragically early age of 49.

Below: 1940 Continental convertible coupe, inspired in 1938 by Edsel Ford's wish for a personalized convertible with a distinctly European look. Right: a 1941 example.

1946

CHRYSLER TOWN & COUNTRY

Wallace's wooden wonder

Although America went to war at the end of 1941 most of the car makers built some models in 1942. One of the most memorable cars of this twilight year was Chrysler's Town and Country, the work of Dave Wallace, on the Windsor chassis. The exposed woodwork resulted in the model being known as a 'Woodie', with the body style being Chrysler's contribution to the growing trend for station wagons. The model was offered almost exclusively in 250 cid (4 liters) six cylinder form with passenger accommodation for six or nine. A total of 996 was built before the firm switched to war production. The theme was revived for 1946 but the station wagon was discontinued and the distinctive woodwork offered on saloons and convertibles in 250 cid (4 liters) six and 323 cid (5.2 liters) eight cylinder versions. There were also a few two door coupés, roadsters and hardtops. In 1948 the six cylinder 'Woodie' was dropped and two years later there was just one version left, the Newport. This was a straight eight powered hardtop but was heavy at 4,670 lbs, so it was progressively fitted with four wheel disc brakes, courtesy of the Chrysler Crown Imperial. The cars that were once marketed as having 'the grace and elegance of a yacht' were dropped in 1950 even though the model had received Fluidrive automatic transmission the previous year. Only 1,299 examples were built in 1950, the Town and Country name being transferred to all-steel station wagons.

Introduced in 1941, the Town and Country models on the Windsor chassis were available in four door form. Production re-started in 1946 when the Town the Country became a model in its own right. Above and middle right dates from this year. Top right: 1947 version while a 1948 County Convertible features right.

CADILLAC SERIES 62

The trendsetting fin

The 1950s were dominated by the tailfin, for manufacturers were following in the wheel tracks of the 1948 Cadillac. The inspiration for the feature came after Harley Earl (General Motors' head of Art and Color section) and his team viewed the still secret P38 Lockheed Lightning pursuit fighter, prior to Pearl Harbor. This came about because GM had supplied the P38's Allison engines. Its twin tail booms made an immediate and lasting impact on the team, which included Earl himself, Bill Mitchell and Frank Hershey. The feature, along with aircraft type cockpits and a propeller nose shape, began appearing in GM's styling mock ups. Maybe we should be thankful that only the fins survived,

having been introduced on the 1948 Series 62 models. The use of fins represented a deliberate attempt by the stylists to provide the rear of the car with its own identity. By paying this sort of attention, whereby the back of the automobile became just as important, stylistically, as its front, yet another all-important Cadillac characteristic was established. The Series 62 was powered by an L head 346 cid (5.6 liter) V8, but the following year saw the introduction of the division's new 331 cid (5.4 liters) overhead valve engine. These two advantages, one stylistic and the other mechanical, underpinned Cadillac's growing sales in the luxury market. In 1946 the division had built 28,144; cars, by 1950 this had risen to 110,535, and two decades later the figure had climbed to over 266,000. With the demise of its old Packard rival in 1958, Cadillac's supremacy was assured.

Above: Cadillac set the post war styling pace with the befinned 1948 models. This is the popular Series 62 with distinctive rear fenders displaying the fins that were to dominate American styling for the next 12 or so years.

1948
TUCKER

Preston's bizarre package

Without doubt, one of the weirdest confections to appear in the American post-war years, the Tucker was introduced in 1948. However, the original 1946 version bore little relation to the sedan that finally emerged two years later. Preston T. Tucker, along with Alex Tremulis, a former Auburn-Duesenberg-Cord stylist, originally intended the car to be powered by a massive 544 cid (9.7 liters) flat six engine incorporating fuel injection and hydraulically operated valve gear with drive taken to the rear wheels via twin torque converters. In addition, there were disc brakes and all-independent suspension, not to mention front wings that turned with the wheels and central steering. Many of these features did not appear on the production Tucker — if there was such a thing. Eventually, a 335 cid (5.5 liters) rear-mounted power unit was employed. This was an air-cooled (subsequently converted to water-cooled) flat six, courtesy of Air Cooled Motors

of Syracuse, New York, which had previously been used to power Bell helicopters. The four door sedan sported all-independent rubber suspension and there was a distinctive central headlight. Transmission was either manual, pre-selector or automatic. The cars were assembled in a former Chrysler airplane engine factory in Chicago, but only 49 cars were produced by 1948 before this 120 mph vehicle, the fastest American model of its day, ceased production. Preston Tucker, in the meantime, had become embroiled in a battle with the Securities and Control Commission over alleged financial irregularities, but he was cleared of these charges in 1950. He then planned to build a small car in Brazil, but while negotiations were under way he fell ill and died of lung cancer in 1956 at the age of 53.

Below: The extraordinary Tucker built in Chicago between 1948 and 1950. The presence of the rear mounted engine will be apparent by the air intakes on the rear fenders.

1953

CHEVROLET CORVETTE

Glass fiber sportster

The influx of European sports cars on the American market, small as it was in the early 1950s, produced a response from General Motors, though the specifications of the original Chevrolet Corvette left much to be desired. It was very much the brainchild of Harley Earl, head of the Corporation's Art and Color studio, and Ed Cole, Chevrolet's Chief Engineer and destined to head GM as President in 1967/74. Earl's stylists were responsible for the convertible glass fiber bodywork, while the car was engineered by Robert McLean, a recent GM recruit. At this stage Chevrolet was still lacking a V8, so the Corvette, named after a fast naval escort vessel, was powered by a 235 cid (3.8 liters) overhead valve six. But the model's most controversial feature was its standardized Powerglide two speed automatic gearbox, which did not exactly help sales take off in the 1953 introductory year, as only 300 examples were sold. The following year was rather better, when 3,640 were produced. It seems likely that with such low production figures the model might have been discontinued had it not been for the appearance of the rival two seater Ford Thunderbird, so GM gritted its corporate teeth and hoped things would improve. They did. In 1955 came the option of a 265 cid (4.3 liters) V8 and practically all cars were so fitted. The restyling for 1956 presented a new purposeful front end, a concave side sculpture, and a three speed manual gearbox, though the automatic remained an option. At last sales began to move and they exceeded 10,000 for the first time in 1960. The model was impressively restyled for 1963. The Sting Ray era had arrived.

The 1953 Chevrolet Corvette represented General Motors's first foray into glass fiber bodywork. Sales were low but GM held on and the model progressed to become an integral part of the performance motoring scene. The example was formerly owned by movie star John Wayne.

Good looks but not sales

The jet engine theme was the overriding feature of the Studebakers introduced in 1950. The styling was the responsibility of Raymond Loewy Associates. Details had already been foreshadowed in the 1949 Fords, to which some Studebaker stylists had lent an unofficial hand. The model line up comprised the short wheelbase Champion and longer Commander and Land Cruiser. The Champion was by far and away the best seller, with an impressive 270,694 built in the first year. In 1951 the Commander received a new 232 cid (3.8 liters) V8, in 1951, while the Champion continued with its 169 cid (2.7 liters) six. In 1952, Studebaker's centenary year (the firm having started life as a

wagon manufacturer), the bullet nose gave way to a new, broad grille, and in the following year the famous Commander and Champion Starliner and Starlight coupes appeared. In 1954 Ford and Chevrolet embarked on a head-on sales battle, and although at first one did no great harm to the other. The few remaining independent manufacturers were the ones who suffered. As production dropped, Studebaker's manufacturing costs soared. In the same year the Champion was updated visually and offered with the Commander's 259 cid (4.2 liters) V8, though by then its own L head six had been increased to 185 cid (3 liters). The Champion, however, had disappeared by 1959 and the last American built Studebaker left the factory in 1964. Despite the take-over of the firm by Packard in 1954, the last Studebaker was built in Canada in 1966.

Arguably the best looking American car of the 1950s, these famous coupes were the responsibility of the Loewy Studios and were the work of Robert E. Bourke, who was based at Studebaker's South Bend, Indiana works. A 1953 Commander Regal Starlighter coupe features.

KAISER MANHATTAN

A challenge that failed

The last attempt to break the tripartite domination of General Motors, Ford, and Chrysler occurred with the arrival of the Frazer and Kaiser marques in 1946. Henry J. Kaiser was a war hero who had successfully mass produced ships during the conflict, he was joined by Joseph W. Frazer of Graham-Paige. Production was centered on the former B-24 bomber factory at Willow Run, Ypsilanti, Michigan, where Ford had mass produced Liberators at the rate of 500 a month. Although the prototype Kaiser featured front wheel drive, unitary body construction and torsion bar suspension, the production models were conventional enough

front-engined/rear wheel drive offerings, powered by a 226 cid (3.7 liters) six cylinder L head engine by Graham-Paige out of Continental. Styling was by Robert Cadwallader who refined Howard Darrin's original concept. The Frazer Manhattan was the more expensive of the two models and, although there was a facelift in 1951, Frazer departed and the make terminated. The Manhattan name was then transferred to Kaiser, where it became the top of the range model. With a move to Toledo, Ohio, the 1954 cars were skillfully restyled by Buzz Grisinger. But the old 226 six was getting long in the tooth, and there was no V8 waiting in the wings, so the Manhattan was offered with a McCulloch centrifugal supercharger which boosted output to 140 bhp. US production ceased in 1955 but the Manhattan dies were shipped to Argentina and the model reappeared there in 1958 as the Kaiser Carabela, where it lasted until 1962.

The Manhattan was Kaiser's best selling model and was available in two and four door forms. A 1953 example features, above right, while a rarer 1954 car is shown above and right.

PACKARD CARIBBEAN

A great firm's sunset

Although Packard had succeeded in weathering the Depression years, by the 1950s it was having to fend off a formidable and ultimately fateful challenge from Cadillac. In 1952, Packard's President, the ageing Hugh Ferry, stepped down, and his place was taken by James Nance, who decided on a positive restatement of the make's upmarket and luxury image. For 1953 he brought in the opulent Caribbean convertible with L head straight eight engine of 327 cid (5.3 liters) and 180 bhp. There were 750 sold in this first year, even with a $5,210 price tag. In 1954 the still profitable Packard bought the ailing Studebaker company with the savior destined to suffer a quick death at the hands of its new partner. This was a disastrous year for Packard,

with just over 27,000 cars produced, though matters improved in 1955 when close to 70,000 Packards found owners. This was the last year that the luxurious Caribbean was produced — about 500 were sold — with all Packard models benefiting from a new 352 cid (5.7 liters) V8 of 275 bhp. In addition, there was Torsion Level suspension system, a sophisticated inter-linked system which provided an outstanding ride and greatly improved handling. The Caribbean's bodywork was much the same as previously though there was a new grille, fenders and rear lights. By this time the model's price had risen to $5,932. But in 1956 only 10,317 Packards were sold and Nance resigned the following year. 1958's Packards were the last; as it was, they were just warmed up Studebakers, and that make only lingered on until 1966, having previously transferred manufacturing operations to Canada.

A Packard in the spirit of the Lincoln Continental, the Caribbean, introduced in 1953. It lasted in this form until 1955. The model was re-styled for 1956 but only remained in production for one year.

CHRYSLER C300

Horse power and high hopes

In 1954 Chrysler was running a poor third behind General Motors and Ford, but the following year it introduced the visually impressive Flight Sweep styling, along with a new 300 series hardtop coupe competitive with the Ford Thunderbird. The well proportioned — almost understated — styling was the work of former Studebaker stylist Virgil Exner, who had joined Chrysler in 1949. The company had inaugurated its potentially potent 'Hemi' V8 in 1951, and by the time that it had been introduced in the C300, it was of 331 cid (5.4 liters) and 300 bhp — the latter figure being echoed in the title. The engine used mechanical rather than hydraulic tappets, a special camshaft and deep breathing twin four barrel carburetors. With this impressive

power output it came as no surprise to find that the model dominated NASCAR racing during 1955 and 1956, despite sales reaching only 1,725 in the first boom year of 1955, which were the best 12 months for the Chrysler marque. In 1956 came the 300B with 340 bhp 354 cid (5.8 liters) and the C300 appeared in 1957. This was visually and mechanically different, incorporating the twin headlamped front end from an Exner ideas car while torsion bar front suspension was introduced to the 1957 Chrysler range with improved road holding. This was the best year for the series, with 1,918 examples sold, and a newly introduced convertible version found 484 owners. However, the 1959 300E's new 413 cid (6.7 liters) V8 was allegedly less of a performer than its 'Hemi' forebears. The 300 line continued through to 1965, three years after Exner had left the Chrysler Corporation.

Seemingly out of place in the glitter of the 1950s, the Chrysler 300 coupe was a low production, potent hardtop coupe with a 300 bhp version of the make's famous 'Hemi' V8 under its hood. This is a 1955 car, the model's introductory year.

FORD THUNDERBIRD

Short lived two seater

Ford's answer to the glass fiber bodied Chevrolet Corvette was the Thunderbird, introduced in 1955. The model had a long gestation period and its birthplace was, of all locations, the 1951 Paris Motor Show. It was there that Ford's General Manager, Lewis D. Crusoe, along with stylist George Walker, decided that they wanted a car in the manner of the European two seaters. Outside consultant Walker and in-house Frank Q. Hershey began work on styling the car, which was accelerated by the arrival of the Corvette in 1953. It was eventually Hershey's profile that was chosen, and he was enthusiastically aided in his work by Bill

Boyer, a young assistant. The car arrived in 1955: an open two seater with a 292 cid (4.7 liters) Mercury V8 under its hood. But the car did not really come up to sales expectations and only 16,155 were sold in the first year. Because of complaints about trunk accommodation, the spare wheel was carried Lincoln-style outside the car from 1956. There was also an optional hardtop with distinctive port holes. 1957 saw a modest restyling with tailfins, and engine options included a 312 cid (5.2 liters) version which had been available since 1956, but with a supercharger and 300 bhp on tap. This was the Thunderbird's best year, with 21,380 built, but Robert McNamara, Ford's Divisional General Manager, felt that demand was insufficient to justify producing the model in its two seater form. So from 1958 the Thunderbird became a rather anonymous four seater. Sales did indeed increase, which put the final nail in the coffin of the two seater Ford.

The origins of Ford's performance image of the 1960s can be found rooted in the two seater Thunderbird of the previous decade. The model was introduced in 1955 as right, with optional hardtop. Below: As from 1956 the spare wheel was carried outside the car.

CONTINENTAL MARK 11

Two door exclusive luxury

With Ford making money again in the 1950s, it was decided to create a new Continental division from 1955 to produce a luxury model to compete head-on with Cadillac. The name Continental was chosen to echo the exclusive nature of the original Lincoln model of 1940, and a division was set up, headed by William Clay Ford, Edsel's youngest son. The two door coupe was a noticeably restrained design in an era renowned for its styling excesses and was the work of an impressive trio of talent: John Renhart, Gordon Buehrig and Bob Thomas. The latter day Continental also retained the spirit of the 1940 original by mounting the spare

wheel vertically in the trunk and silhouetting its outline in the lid. This luxury model was powered by a specially assembled 368 cid (6 liters) Lincoln V8 mated to a Multi Drive three speed automatic transmission. The car was put on sale in 1956 for $10,000, but with sales of only 1,325 Ford lost $1,000 on every one it built. Things were even worse in the following year, with only 444 Continentals sold, and for 1958 the model's price was drastically slashed to $5,825. But by this time it was too late. For 1958 Ford had decided to introduce a Mark III Continental, with plenty of chrome, large fenders and fins. A four model range was offered and sales perked up, also helped by the provision of a larger 430 cid (7 liters) V8. However, the Continental division merged with Lincoln-Mercury for 1959 and until 1968 the Continental model name reverted to Lincoln.

Following in the wheel tracks of the original 1940 Lincoln Continental, the 1956 Continental reflected the booming 1950s though, alas, it failed to sell in the expected quantities. It was replaced by a marginally more successful Mark III car in 1958.

If you could not quite run to a Continental Mark II, then how about the exclusive Dual-Ghia? This is the original Dodge based Firebomb model of 1955, powered by a 317 cid (5.2 liter) V8.

DODGE CUSTOM ROYAL

Exner looks ahead

Dodge, a member of the Chrysler Corporation since 1928, was producing some notably unsensational cars in the early 1950s. Styling fortunately improved and in 1956 Virgil Exner's designs sprouted the almost obligatory tail fins. The 1957 Dodges were all new and sported the so-called Forward look, which, although awash with fins and chrome, did not topple over into the vulgarity of 1958's Oldsmobiles. The luxurious Royal range dated back to 1954 and the following year introduced the more expensive Custom Royal with 183 bhp 270 cid (4.4 liters) V8 and 193 bhp option. By 1956 the Custom Royal was being offered with a larger

315 cid (5.1 liters) V8, and the 1957 four model line up consisted of a four door sedan, Lancer hardtop sedan and coupe, and convertible coupe. A total of 55,149 Custom Royals were sold in 1957, which was a modest improvement over the previous year. Transmission was a Powerglide automatic while the torsion bar independent front suspension answered to the name of Torsion-Aire. The 3,690 lb and the 260 bhp of the 325 cid (5.3 liters) V8 were arrested by Total Contact anti-dive brakes, but for 1958 the potent and pricy 'Hemi' was replaced by a cheaper 350 cid (5.7 liters) unit. Sales subsequently declined and by 1959 the Custom Royal series had come to the end of the road despite the arrival of a 361 cid (5.9 liters) power unit. In its final year a mere 21,206 examples of the series were sold.

The Dodge Custom Royal was one of the better styled cars to arrive amongst the glitter and chrome of the 1950s. The first year's production was the best but demand fell away until the model was discontinued in 1959.

ELDORADO BROUGHAM

Cadillac's lavish hardtop

In 1955 America produced an astounding 7.9 million cars, nearly double the 1948 level and not to be surpassed until 1965. No car more typifies the optimism and extravagance of the mid 1950s than the Cadillac Eldorado Brougham, intended to appeal to a rich but discriminating clientele. The car made its public debut at the 1955 General Motors Motorama but did not enter production until the end of 1956 with an eyebrow raising $13,074 price tag. It was a pillarless four door sedan with distinctive brushed aluminium roof, a favorite Harley Earl feature, and twin headlamps, an innovation it shared with Nash and which the rest

of the industry were soon to copy. A 364 cid (5.9 liters) V8 engine supplied 325 bhp, but less conventional was the air suspension which produced a magnificently smooth ride when it was working properly. The system had been used on commercial vehicles since 1952 but was refined when embodied in the Eldorado's specification, and there were leakages, an unforgivable failing on such an expensive car. A mere 704 examples were sold in two years despite the fact that the model offered Hydra-Matic automatic transmission, power assisted steering, brakes, while the seats could be electrically controlled. Electric operation of the windows and trunk lid were other noteworthy features. In view of the poor sales figures for 1959 the Brougham was completely restyled by Pinin Farina and the bodies produced by them in Italy. That was even less successful than the original version and only 200 had been built by the time output ceased in 1960.

Cadillac occasionally gets it wrong and its Eldorado Brougham was a case in point. But what a fabulous extravagance it was. Like the Continental Mark II, the two door Brougham was aimed at the very rich but despite the Cadillac name and all too obvious luxury, the model did not sell.

CHEVROLET BEL AIR

Best selling beauty

The hardtop look reached Chevrolet in 1950 in the shape of the Bel Air version of the De Luxe Styleline range, a two door offering, though the roof remained firmly in place. The engine was an L head six of 216 cid (3.5 liters) so performance was hardly sensational, and remained so until 1955, with the arrival of Chevrolet's 265 cid (4.3 liters) overhead valve V8. Such were the advances in design and engine construction that the new power unit, although boasting two extra cylinders, was lighter than the long-running six it replaced. Upon the demise of the Styleline range in 1953, the Bel Air became a model name in its own right

and there was a styling facelift in 1955. From then until 1957 production boomed and over six million Chevrolets of all types were built. There had been another styling revision in 1956 and a further one in 1957, while the following year's cars were bigger and slower than their predecessors. The robust '57 Chevrolet was really in need of replacement; this was reflected by Ford being a mere 130 cars behind the make in that year's output figures. Of the 1957 Bel Air range the four door version was the most popular, production reaching an impressive quarter of a million plus, even the convertible sold a respectable 47,562. Engines began with a 235 cid (3.8 liters) L head six; 235 cid and 283 cid (4.6 liters) versions were also offered. The latter was available in a horse power range from 185 to 283, the exact displacement of the V8 in cubic inches.

Although the 1957 Chevrolet Bel Air was most popular in four door sedan form, there was also a hardtop sports coupe and a convertible coupe of the type shown. These fins, thankfully, are within reasonable proportions.

FORD SKYLINER

Switch to open air

It was in 1955 that the Fairlane series, named after Ford's Dearborn estate, took over from the Crestline as the most expensive car in the company's four model line up. Engines were a 223 cid (3.6 liters) and the firm's new 272 cid (4.4 liters) V8, introduced in 1954. In 1957 came the Skyliner that at first sight looked like a conventional convertible, but was fitted with an automatic retractable hardtop. The feature had been originally conceived as a fitment on the Continental Mark II but it was decided to offer the idea on the top of range Fairlane. A total of $20 million was lavished on the project, as the complicated system operated electrically, involving over 600 feet of wiring, 10 power relays, 10 limit switches, three electric motors and eight circuit breakers. This permitted the roof to be stowed under the car's rear decking that opened, like a great mouth, to receive it, and having 'digested' it would then close. The system would only work when the automatic gearbox was in neutral so that the operation could not be carried out with the car in motion. The most expensive model of the Fairlane range, the Skyliner, sold for $2,942, which was $347 more than the standard convertible that it so closely resembled. In view of the extra weight it was powered by the 272 cid (4.4 liters) V8, which was optional for the rest of the range. During the first year 20,766 examples were sold, but sales fell off and the option was discontinued in 1959. This piece of automotive one-upmanship suffered from limited luggage space while electrical failures, notwithstanding a crank handle mechanical override, were embarrassing to owners. A total of 48,394 Skyliners were built.

It no doubt seemed a good idea at the time but the Ford Skyliner never really caught the public imagination and was the low seller in the Fairlane 500 range. Sales of around 20,000 per annum in 1957 progressively declined and only 12,915 examples were sold in 1959, its final production year. Nevertheless the Skyliner is a revealing echo of the gadget orientated opulence of the 1950s.

MERCURY TURNPIKE CRUISER

Downhill all the way

It was in 1938 that Ford launched its Mercury division to challenge General Motors impressive model line up. The Mercury was, in effect, a Ford with a different and more expensive body, intended to slot in between the cheap models providing value for money and the exclusive low-production Lincolns. During the first year the cars were known as Ford-Mercurys but the parental prefix was dropped in 1940. By 1950 Mercury was well established as a make in its own right, the millionth example being built in that year. The cars were V8-powered from the outset and, like Ford, went to an overhead valve engine in 1954, and a 368 cid (6 liters) version was used under the massive hood of the Mercury Turnpike Cruiser of 1957. This was offered in two and four door

hardtop and convertible forms and its name reflected a spate of toll road highway building that was taking place in America in the 1950s. The styling, however, derived from the Ford XM dream car of the same name, represented an uneasy combination of styles. There were fins, sculptured rear quarter panels and an enclosed spare wheel carried Lincoln fashion outside the trunk, and that was only the rear… Twin headlamps and a garish grille completed the package. Unfortunately for Ford, the model's launch coincided with the market taking a tumble in 1957/8, Mercury dropped from a 1955 seventh place to eighth in the sales league. 1957's Turnpike sales were only 16,861 and, not surprisingly, the model was discontinued. Despite a reappearance in toned-down form in 1958, it had sunk without trace by the end of the year.

The Turnpike Cruiser, though positively groaning with chrome, fins and other ill assorted features was a poor seller and was only built in 1957. It was powered by a 368 cid (6 liter) V8 which was also offered as an option on the rest of the Mercury range.

EDSEL CITATION/PACER

Ford's lost division

The Edsel's origins are rooted in the boom year of 1955 as part of an attempt by Ford to challenge the Dodge, Pontiac and Buick middle ground. A new division was established which took the name of Edsel, Ford senior's eldest son and Henry Ford II's father. This was after the company had rejected a host of names, some even emanating from New York poetess Marianne Moore, hired by the company for the purpose. The new car was unveiled in September 1957 in Ranger, Pacer, Corsair and Citation versions, with 361 cid (5.9 liters) and 410 cid (6.7 liters) V8 engine options. An automatic transmission was available with its press buttons on the steering wheel spokes: a novel feature. The styling was by Roy Brown — later to be responsible for the 1962 British Ford

Cortina — and reflected current trends, though the 'horse's collar' radiator grille was noteworthy. Unfortunately the Edsel range coincided with a slump and the projected 1958 sales of 100,000 failed to materialize; a mere 63,110 Edsels were sold. It was much the same story for 1959 but a complete collapse came in 1960, with only a Station Wagon (introduced the previous year) and Ranger line ups being offered. It was even possible to have a 300 bhp 'Super Express' V8 for a mere $58 extra. That season's sales amounted to just 3,008 cars, though the Edsel division itself had been wound up at the end of the previous year. But by 1960 Ford was pushing ahead with its Falcon and Comet compact models and the demise of the Edsel was overtaken by their success. Ford is reckoned to have lost $350 million in the project; a tragedy. Edsel Ford deserved a better memorial.

Named after Henry Ford 1's eldest son, the Edsel division was created by Ford to capture, unsuccessfully as it proved, the middle ground. 1958 was the first year of production and both these cars date from this year. The 361 cid (5.9 liter) Pacer hardtop is shown on the left while the Citation convertible (there were only 930 built that year) displays the model's distinctive radiator grille.

1959
PONTIAC BONNEVILLE

Knudsen moves ahead

When Edward Murphy began producing cars in Pontiac. Michigan, in 1907 he called his make Oakland, which was taken over by General Motors in 1909. It was not until 1926 that a cheaper Pontiac car was introduced, but it soon overhauled Oakland, so the latter make was discontinued in 1931. The town from which the car took its title was named after a famous Indian chief, a representation serving as the make's mascot. Pontiac and Oldsmobile regularly swapped places in the GM production league up to the 1950s, although Oldsmobile forged ahead in 1954. It remained there until 1959, when Pontiac decisively moved ahead, and during the 1960s stayed in third place, with only

Chevrolet and Ford producing more cars. This transformation in the division's affairs was set in motion by the appointment in 1956 of Sermon E. 'Bunkie' Knudsen, who at 43 was the youngest of the corporation's general managers. Although the 1958 Pontiacs almost rivalled the Oldsmobiles for vulgarity, the 1959 cars appeared with ornament much reduced and a distinctive split radiator grille introduced. The Catalina, Star Chief and Bonneville models were available, with the latter selling close on 82,000 examples during its first year. A 389 cid (6.3 liters) V8 was provided throughout the range, with horsepower options varying between 215 and 310, the last named in Tri-Power form. A new, so-called Wide Track chassis was employed. For those who required economy there was the 420E which, when driven with care, could return 20 miles per gallon, effectively anticipating the energy-conscious 1970s.

The 1959 Bonneville was a great visual improvement over the previous year's Pontiac excesses. This Sport Hardtop Coupe was second only to the Vista Hardtop Sedan in popularity.

1963
CHEVROLET CORVAIR

Sting in a Compact's tail

Just as the Chevrolet Corvette was produced in response to European sports cars, so the division's Corvair was intended to stem the flow of small car imports, headed by the Volkswagen Beetle. The model was technically adventurous for an American car and echoed the German newcomer with a rear-mounted air-cooled 140 cid (2.2 liters) flat six engine, all-independent suspension with coils and wishbones at the front and a swing axle rear. Top of the range was the Monza, with luxurious interior and bucket seats and selling only 11,926 in the 1960 introductory year. Sales accelerated in 1961 after the introduction of an optional four speed manual gearbox, and over 140,000 found owners. The same year the Corvair's engine capacity was upped to 145 cid (2.3 liters), and capacity was increased again to 164 cid (2.7 liters) in 1964. There was also a turbocharged version of the Monza offered in Spyder (open) form. For 1965 the Corvair was facelifted, when William Mitchell provided a crisp re-skinning. Simultaneously the rear suspension was revised to a fully independent layout in view of criticism relating to the basic swing axle. By this time the model was having to face the formidable challenge of the Ford Mustang, while the knock-out blow was provided by Ralph Nader's *Unsafe at Any Speed,* published in 1965, in which the model was severely criticized. The model lasted until 1969, two years after its creator, Ed Cole, had been elevated to the Presidency of General Motors.

The Corvair Monza was far more successful than the standard Corvair sedan and coupe that inspired its creation. Introduced in 1960, the convertible (Spyder) followed in 1962.

BUICK RIVIERA

Putting on the style

Buick had been a member of the General Motors conglomerate since William Durant founded it in 1908. During the inter-war years the marque attained an upper middle class image and until the mid 1950s continued to hold its own. But thereafter demand dipped and in 1959 Edward Rollert was brought in to the division to revive falling sales. This he succeeded in doing and the Riviera, introduced to challenge Ford's four seater Thunderbird, was representative of the new approach. This sports coupe, superbly styled by Bill Mitchell, who had taken over from Harley Earl as head of GM's Art and Color department in 1958, had a

clean clipped profile that represented a marked contrast to the flamboyance of the previous decade. The origins of the style can be found in a convertible which appeared at General Motors 1955 Motorama, created with a view to reviving the pre-war La Salle marque. This was never undertaken, though traces of it can be found in the Riviera, along with the influence of British razor edge styling. It was offered intially with the most powerful of the V8 range, a 401 cid (6.6 liters) engine which was upped to 415 cid (6.8 liters) in 1964. The model continued to evolve for the next decade and although a 1971 facelift was successful — its rear end reminiscent of the Chevrolet Corvette — the 1974 re-think presented a less distinctive offering. Although a Buick Riviera is still made, this front wheel drive model has nothing in common with its forebears, apart from its very marketable name.

Above: The Buick Riviera of 1963 used a 401 cid (6.6 liter) V8 engine, the largest capacity unit then available to the make. An impressive 40,000 examples were produced in the first year which was not bettered until 1966.

STUDEBAKER AVANTI

Loewy moves forward

The Avanti was Studebaker's swansong but it was an impressive note on which to bow out. Sterwood Egbert, who became Studebaker's President in 1961, asked master stylist Raymond Loewy to design a memorable sports car to revitalize the make. The Avanti, Italian for 'forward,' was built around a shortened Studebaker Lark frame with a 240 bhp V8 of 289 cid (4.7 liters) and Paxton supercharger as a standard fitment. There was an optional 290 bhp variant. The two door glass fiber bodywork was notable for its apparent absence of a radiator grille, air entering via a scoop positioned below the front fender. The car entered production in 1963 but there was a powerful challenge in the shape of William Mitchell's revamped Chevrolet Corvette: the Avanti at $4,445 cost $193 more, and there were problems with curing the glass fiber body. Consequently, only 3,834 Avantis were produced in 1963, compared with 21,513 Corvettes. There was an optional increase in engine capacity, to 304 cid (4.9 liters), but this made little difference and only 819 Avantis were sold in 1964. This, it seemed, spelled the end of the model, but Leo Newman and Nathan Altmann, partners in the oldest Studebaker dealership in the country, bought the car outright together with a portion of the South Bend, Indiana, factory. The outcome, in 1965, was Avanti II, though the engine was the Chevrolet Corvette V8, and this model is still in production at the time of writing (1984), 21 years after it first appeared.

Below: Raymond Loewy's famous styling studio had not influenced Studebaker's looks since 1956 but their presence returned with the outstanding glass fiber Avanti of 1963. Unfortunately there were production problems and enthusiastic prospective purchasers probably opted for a Chevrolet Corvette.

PONTIAC GTO

Flexing of muscles

Pontiac borrowed Ferrari's GTO initials ('Gran Turismo Omologato', which means roughly, Competition High Speed Tourer) for its big engined Tempest of 1964. Judged as one of the first of the so-called Muscle Cars, it was the result of Jim Wangers, an account executive with D'Arcy McManus who handled Pontiac's business, shoe horning a 389 cid (6.3 liters) V8 into a two door Tempest Le Mans coupe. This gave the GTO a top speed of around the 130 mark and Pontiac thought that they might sell about 5,000 of them. Other GTO specialities, available at extra cost, were high geared steering, uprated shock absorbers, twin exhausts and special tires. It was also possible to specify a 348 bhp version of the V8 for another $115. It was only after sales exceeded 32,000 in the first year that Pontiac realized it might have a winner on its hands, so for 1965 horsepower was increased from 325 to 335 and there was a top line 360. Sales again soared, with over 75,000 GTOs sold. For 1966 the model's appeal was broadened with a hardtop and convertible joining the coupe. In addition to the V8s, an overhead camshaft six with 207 bhp was available. Engines got even bigger and in 1970 the GTO was fitted with a 455 cid (7.4 liters) V8 which developed 366 bhp. But with the trend to smaller engines in the 1970s, the GTO's days were numbered and the model was discontinued in 1973. The following year the GTO name was applied to the Ventura compact car, a total contradiction of objectives, and only about 7,000 were made before the GTO name disappeared from the Pontiac model line up.

First of the so called Muscle Cars, the Pontiac GTO of 1964 was available in hardtop, sport and convertible coupe forms with the latter variation, shown here, sold 6,644 examples in its introductory year.

1965

FORD MUSTANG

Iacocca's jackpot

The Mustang has the distinction of having the fastest first year sales of any car in the history of the American automobile industry. Creator and driving force of the concept was Lee Iacocca, who took over from Robert McNamara as General Manager of the Ford division in 1960. Iacocca recognized that the post-war baby boom was due to peak in the 1960s and realized that Ford's product line did not meet the sporty requirements of the young buyer. At this stage he did not quite know what he did want–though he knew it was not the mid-engined Mustang I, completed in 1962 as an experimental project and too sophisticated for mass production. Mustang II, by contrast, was a racy coupe, with stylist Joe Oros capturing exactly the image that Iacocca was looking for. This prototype was duly exhibited at the 1963 American Grand Prix and the car went into production in 1964, being launched that April in coupe and convertible, forms with the fastback following later in the year. Standard fitment was a 170 cid (2.7 liters) six, though optional V8s were available. Ford's original forecast was 100,000 sales in the first year, but prior to the model's launch, Iacocca upped the figure to 240,000. As it happened, it took just four months for the Mustang to reach the 100,000 figure, with the 250,000th example sold in seven. By the end of the 1965 model year no less than 680,992 cars had been sold. Performance wizard Carroll Shelby produced a potent 428 cid (7 liters) version and the original concept remained in production until 1973. Although a Mustang is still listed in Ford's model line up, subsequent versions have never displayed the sales acceleration of the original.

Ford's Mustang was the fastest selling car in the history of the American motor industry until the arrival of the General Motors X-cars in 1980. Above: 1964 Mustang with the World War II fighter aircraft which shares the same name. Right and above: is the Shelby GT-350 Mustang produced in addition to a GT-500 car with 428 cid (7 liter) V8.

OLDSMOBILE TORONADO

Pull instead of push

American motor manufacturers largely were shy of front wheel drive until the arrival of the General Motors X-car range of 1980. Therefore, when Oldsmobile announced its Toronado in 1966, which featured this configuration, it was something of a mechanical curiosity, but a very impressive one at that. When it was conceived, the intention was to combine the traditional American attributes of smoothness and power from a big-bored V8 with the road holding and tractive advantages of front wheel drive. A split transmission system, with the gearbox and torque converter, connected by chain drive, permitted the engine to be carried well forward, resulting in good weight distribution, so the

stylish coupe handled and performed well, having a top speed of well over 130 mph. The engine was a 385 bhp 425 cid (6.9 liters) V8, which was shared with other rear-drive Oldsmobiles. As the Toronado was a top line model, selling for $4,366 in De Luxe hardtop coupe form, sales of 34,630 in the first year were respectable and, in 1967, Cadillac adopted the Toronado's front wheel drive layout for its Eldorado, though incorporating its own William Mitchell styled coupe body. By 1972 engine sizes were in decline and the Toronado's V8 output was down to 265 bhp, to comply with emission controls and safety regulations. By this time front wheel disc brakes had been introduced and the coupe shape continued until 1978, when it was replaced by a more compact design, still retaining the Toronado name and, of course, front wheel drive.

America's first mass produced front wheel drive car, the 1966 Oldsmobile Toronado, produced only in hardtop coupe form was as impressive as it was unconventional. The mechanical layout was shared with the Cadillac Eldorado of the following year.

1968
DODGE CHARGER R/T

Fast and furious

America's car makers became increasingly aware of the importance of a performance image, particularly amongst the younger generation, in the 1960s. Dodge responded to this need in 1966 with the Charger, a fastback coupe version of the mid range Coronet and largely conceived with a view to winning stock car events. It was initially powered by a 318 cid (5.2 liters) V8, and 37,344 examples were sold in the first year. In 1966 the Charger had a runaway success in NASCAR contests, winning 18 events and keeping well ahead of the opposition. For the following year there was a new 440 cid (7.2 liters) V8 engine, and in 1968 the Charger was restyled to the improvement of its looks. The R/T model was particularly popular and Charger sales rose that year to 96,108. Even though the new Charger was capable of

an impressive 184 mph, the Fords were faster on the circuits and in 1968 the model only managed five wins. There were a few, mostly visual, changes in 1969, and that year witnessed the arrival of the Charger 500, offered with a 426 cid (6.9 liters) engine as standard and the 440 as an optional fitment. Intended to trounce the opposition on the speedways, the model, unfortunately, failed to come up to expectations, so Dodge pulled out the stops and produced the Charger Daytona, which left the production line ready for the race track and sporting a prominent rear aerofoil. This managed better than the 500, and in 1970 an example achieved 17 NASCAR wins as well as the coveted championship title. When a new body arrived for 1971, Muscle Cars were becoming unfashionable and demand dipped, though the Charger continued to hold its own in competition. Although the model moved up market, by 1978 it was no more, though the memory of its successes on the speedways lives on.

Although the Dodge Charger was derived from the Coronet model, it possessed its own very individual personality. Its concealed headlights were a distinctive feature while the split back seat would fold away and there was an appropriately sporting interior.

PLYMOUTH ROAD RUNNER

A 220mph Superbird

Plymouth, Chrysler's popular low-price make, introduced its intermediate range Belvedere in 1965. Bearing a family resemblance to the larger Fury, it was offered in a variety of two and four door sedan body styles as well as coupe and convertible options. The model was successfully campaigned in NASCAR events and was restyled in 1968. Introduced the same year was the cheaper Road Runner version, named after the popular Warner Brothers' cartoon character. As if to underline the fact that the model's horn produced a distinctive 'beeb beeb' like the flightless bird whose name it bore. More significantly, this was a two door coupe which featured uprated suspension and powered by a 383 cid (6.2 liters) V8 with a 426 cid (6.9 liters) option. A convertible Road Runner arrived for 1969 and there was a special version, the Superbird, similar to the in-house Dodge Charger and Daytona with a 440 cid (7.2 liters) V8 which provided 375 bhp. The Superbird certainly lived up to its name, and during 1970 achieved 21 NASCAR victories which compared with the Road Runner's two wins in 1969, a state of affairs that had prompted the Superbird's hatching. By 1971 the Road Runner was available in hardtop form only with a 383 cid (6.2 liters) V8, though later in the year came a 275 bhp 340 cid (5.6 liters) option. But by 1972 the Road Runner had run its course with the arrival of smaller capacity engines and a corporate clampdown on performance models.

The Superbird variation on the Road Runner theme arrived in 1970, easily identifiable by its distinctive droop snout and impressive rear tailfins which carried a stabliser wing. It needed one. In racing trim the Superbird had a top speed of 220 mph though road going versions were tamer.

1973-1978
CHEVROLET CAMARO

Putting on the power

After the astounding success of the Ford Mustang, General Motors' contribution to the Ponycar stampede was the Chevrolet Camaro, introduced for 1967. A purposeful two door offering in convertible and hardtop forms, the Camaro was listed with a wide variety of power units ranging from 230 cid (3.7 liters) sixes to the 350 cid (5.7 liters) V8. An even larger engine, the 396 cid (6.4 liters) V8, became available in 1967. One of the most celebrated early examples was the Z-28 version conceived with the Sports Car Club of America Trans-American Championship in mind. As the rules stipulated, a 305 cid (5 liters) limit, a 302 cid (4.9 liters)

engine was cooked up from a 327 block and 283 crankshaft. Suspension was modified accordingly and, although the car came third that season behind Ford and Mercury, in 1968 it was victorious and won 10 out of 13 events. These successes encouraged General Motors to revamp the model and, as a result, a single body style, a coupe, looking as though it meant business, arrived for the 1970 season. Top of the engine options was a 402 cid (6.5 liters) V8 available in 375 bhp form in its most powerful version. But it was downhill from 1971 onwards as potential purchasers became more energy-conscious and emission controls were enforced. There was a 1974 facelift and the Camaro continued up until 1981, when the name was transferred to a front wheel drive sports coupe. The great days were over.

Chevrolet's Camaro replaced the Corvair as a firm favorite amongst the young generation of car buyers, right from its 1967 launch. Like Ford's Mustang, it was offered with a variety of engines. In addition there were also no less than 81 mechanical and trim options along with a host of dealer fitted accessories.

1976
CADILLAC
ELDORADO

Detroit baroque

Cadillac first used the Eldorado name to grace a limited production, super luxury convertible in 1953. From that moment on, Eldorados were recognized as rather special Cadillacs: in 1957 the ultra-expensive, hand-built Eldorado Brougham, the distinctive 1959 Eldorado Biarritz, then the 1967 front wheel drive Eldorado hardtop. Besides the revised 1971 hardtop, the Eldorado offered a convertible in 1971, which continued with little change through 1976. Powered by a mammoth 500 cid (8 liter) V8, introduced in 1970, along with the dubious distinction of having the world's largest car engine, the Eldorado convertible spanned an enormous 224.1 inches in length. It was also the only American built convertible left; every other car line had dropped theirs in

the face of increasing safety regulations and buyer resistance. Out of 49,184 Eldorados built in 1976, 14,000 were convertibles. Cadillac made a point of letting everybody know this model would be the last. Assuming this was to be the end of a piece of automotive history, speculators bought Eldorado convertibles as possible collector investments. Standard equipment included leather interior, four wheel disc brakes, automatic level control, folding hide-away top, and air conditioning. Anti-lock braking (rear wheels only) and Bendix electronic fuel injection were available. At $11,049 the 1976 Eldorado convertible was too big and didn't handle as well as the 1967-70 models. After the initial collector interest, this last expression of pure Detroit baroque can be bought today for under its price as new.

Standard equipment on the 1976 Cadillac Eldorado Convertible included folding hide-away top, air conditioning, four wheel disc and antilocking brakes.

STUTZ BLACKHAWK

The ultimate in luxury

For pure, unadulterated extravagance you need look no further than the Stutz Blackhawk. The blame for this excess has to be laid fairly and squarely upon the shoulders of influential stylist Virgil Exner. Exner's designs came to the attention of New York businessman William O'Donnell. Realising their potential he formed the Stutz Motor Car Corporation of America in 1968. With Exner in tow as designer, O'Donnell put the Stutz into very limited production – and at a price he knew would command exclusivity. The Stutz is built on a Pontiac Bonneville base. The 1980 model used Pontiac's 403 cid engine and GM's three-speed

Turbo-Hydra-matic transmission. Today that engine is no longer available and the Stutz is having to make do with a smaller unit. Nothing is done to improve the Pontiac chassis – it is left as it came from the factory. All the effort goes into the bodywork and the interior, which is the ultimate in luxury. All the interior hardware is 24 carat gold-plated, the seats are covered in sensually soft Italian leather, the carpets are made of thick fur and the dashboard is real English walnut. Fake outside exhaust pipes, fake running boards and deck-mounted spare tire add to the flamboyant design. The protruding grille is heavily chromed as are bumpers and door sills. Inside the narrow trunk the floor is covered with sheepskin. The Stutz Blackhawk is assembled by Ghia of Italy and barely three or four dozen are manufactured in any one year.

The ultimate in fabulous luxury – both inside and out – the most expensive model will set you back a cool $300,000.

PONTIAC TRANS-AM

A hell for leather look

Mere mention of this illustrious name Trans-Am conjures up memories to those who were in their late teens or early twenties when Pontiac's answer to the wildly successful Mustang hit the streets, First it was the Firebird, launched late in 1966 as a 1967 model, closely followed by the heavy duty, fire breathing Trans-Am. Based on Chevrolet's Camaro, the Firebird/Trans-Am distinguished itself with a divided grille. A range of engines, from Pontiac's under-rated SOHC six to a 400 cubic inch V8, kept Pontiac's performance image intact. Especially the Trans-Am with its enormous eagle decal splayed across the hood. Throughout the performance depressed seventies, Pontiac's pony-car changed little. Perhaps they weren't as quick but mid to late seventies Trans-Ams handled better and were still able to

induce moderate wheelspin. In 1982 the third generation Trans-Am arrived. The slick, smooth body, uncluttered by superfluous add-ons and trim, is shared with Chevy's Camaro with detail differences to distinguish the two. A 305 cid V8 gave the Trams-Am some poke but it was still fairly lackluster compared with the old. More power arrived in 1983 with the high output 305 coupled to a five speed manual transmission. It began to look as though Pontiac were getting serious about performance again. Come 1985 and the Trans-Am was about to be eclipsed by Camaro's stunning new IROC-Z. A smart new interior, economically designed Recaro style seating, a special paint job plus the flashy eagle decal, gave the Trans-Am a hell for leather look. Underneath all the gloss is the business end of the 1985 Trans-Am. Beneath the hood sits a 305 (5 liter) port injected or 4 barrel V8 developing 190 bhp net. In this guise the Trans-Am can knock off 0-60 in around 7½ seconds. To keep all this power on the road, Pontiac offers its WS6 suspension option. This includes gas-filled shock absorbers, bigger front and rear anti-sway bars, four wheel disc brakes and Goodyear 245/50VR-16 'gatorback tires. In essence it is much the same as the IROC-Z package.

Above and over page: The 1985 Trans-Am can move from standing to 60 mph in about 7½ seconds. From the performance-depressed '70s, Pontiac has given back excitement to the Trans-Am.

1985
FORD MUSTANG

A car for the '80s

Twenty-one years have passed since the first Mustang hit the street, in April 1964. The inspiration of Lee A. Iacocca, then General Manager of Ford division, the Mustang was created as a small 'personal' car with sporty good looks and a range of engine options. Of the six current models available the most talked about is the turbocharged SVO. Introduced in 1984, the SVO is an out and out street racer with handling to match. Powered by a 2.3 liter SOHC turbocharged 4 cylinder engine developing 175 bhp net, it is capable of 130 mph plus. That the car can zoom from standstill to 60 in 7½ seconds and reach such high speeds carrying over 3000 lbs weight, is mostly due to Ford's excellent turbocharger unit. This refined piece of machinery boasts an air-to-air intercooler which drops the air charge intake temperature from 300°F to 175°F, thereby increasing its density. This means greater combustion efficiency and a 20% increase in power. The SVO is very European in concept. It has ergonomically designed seats, complete with adjustable lumbar support, four wheel disc brakes, gas filled adjustable Koni shocks, adjustable rack and pinion power steering and P225/50VR 16 Goodyear Eagle tires. Power front windows, power locks, rear window defroster, AM/FM stereo radio and cassette player and air conditioning are all standard in the SVO's base $15,000 price. The Mustang SVO is undoubtedly an example of American automotive thinking for the eighties and beyond.

All Mustangs are good, but the connoisseur's choice has to be the SVO – named after Ford's Special Vehicles Operations unit.

CHEVROLET CORVETTE

Corvette comes of age

Ever since the legendary Corvette arrived on the scene in 1953, it has established itself as America's only true sportscar. A new look Corvette, the classic split rear window Stingray, arrived in 1963, complete with all round independent suspension. Four wheel disc brakes followed shortly after. New for 1966 was the mighty 427 cid V8 which was further developed to produce a massive 435 bhp in 1967. 1968 found a swoopy new Corvette, replete with fender bulges, taking to the road. Under the hood burbled a 327 V8. The 427 was enlarged to 454 cubic inches for 1970 to compensate for loss of performance, the result of federal mandated emissions controls. From 1971, on power, performance and compression ratios dropped significantly. By 1975, the only engine option of any note was the L82, a 350 cid V8 developing 205 bhp net. Though no longer the shattering performer of old, the Corvette was still able to go 0–60 in a shade over 7 seconds.

Chevrolet spent the rest of the decade refining the Corvette into a luxurious sports tourer. Apart from detail changes to the front and rear ends the fiberglass legend remained much the same for 14 years. Then 1983 saw the arrival of an entirely new Corvette. Described as an '84 model, the new Corvette was launched in March 1983. New from the ground up, the four wheel disc brakes were a new design, power assisted rack and pinion steering replaced the previous recirculating ball type and Goodyear developed the Eagle VR50 'gatorback tire especially for Corvette. A fuel injected 350 V8, mated to either a 4 speed manual or 4 speed automatic, cut 0-60 times to around 6.8 seconds. Beautiful to look at, with handling generally superior to most cars in its class, the '84 Corvette was a deserved hit. For 1985 Chevrolet retuned spring rates and shock valving for a softer ride. To ensure the Corvette's superb handling, one inch wider front wheels were added. With a top speed of almost 150 mph, what more could a sportscar fan want?

The world-class 1985 Corvette, with a top speed of nearly 150 mph, can move from 0 to 60 in an incredible 6.2 seconds.

Above: The ultimate tailpiece from Cadillac.

Back end paper: the fire-breathing '85 Pontiac Trans-Am at speed.

PICTURE CREDITS